A Walking Tour of Rice University

A Rice University Studies

Special Publication

Contents

Preface vii

Introduction xi

The Tour 1

Entrance 1

Lovett Hall 3

Physics Building 19

Sewall Hall 26

Academic Court 28

Anderson Hall 30

Chemistry Building 31

Abercrombie Engineering Laboratory 41

Mechanical Laboratory 43

Ryon Engineering Laboratory 45

Herman Brown Building 46

Hamman Hall 46

Space Science Building 47

Keith-Wiess Geological Laboratories 48

Anderson Biological Laboratories 49

Rice Memorial Student Center and Chapel 51

Fondren Library 55

Rayzor Hall 58

Cohen House 58

Allen Center 67

Residential Colleges 67

Rice Stadium 83

Preface

I happened upon the Rice scene at just the right time. In 1940 William Ward Watkin, who was the architects' representative on the original work and who later designed some of the other buildings himself, was giving slide talks. I was "invited" to run the projector (an elderly 3 1/4" x 4" manual one), changing slides to follow Mr. Watkin's prepared text. How could I possibly fail to become interested? Like all visitors to the Rice campus, I had asked of the various faces and symbols cut in stone, cast in bronze, or molded in clay, "Who are you? What do you represent?" Fortunately I was able, through William Ward Watkin and James Chillman, Jr., to find many of the answers.

I began photographing the campus myself in the late 1940s, but it was not until after Mr. Watkin's death in 1953 that I began conducting campus tours. They were initiated as part of the Faculty Women's Club program for wives of newcomers to the faculty, but I felt especially honored and encouraged by the repeated attendance of Mrs. Dorothy Richter and of Miss Pender Turnbull. I secretly suspect that they both knew as much about the tour as I did but were kind enough not to expose me!

Two problems developed with regard to the guided tours. First, they became so popular that it was impossible for those attending to hear even my basso profundo. Second, they were rather tiring for many people as the walks grew longer and longer. Hence a series of slide talks evolved. These had the obvious advantage of making the tours available to large numbers with less wear and tear on the audiences and of being independent of the weather or the time of day. I would not attempt to guess the number of tours or slide presentations that I have made over the years.

Later, at the urging of the Development Office of the university, Douglas Killgore produced a 16mm sound film called *Rice Today*; but because of its limited coverage, the film simply whets the appetite. In 1981 the Office of Information Services produced the Rice University Calendar, but this also only scratched the surface. After each tour or slide show or presentation of *Rice Today*, members of the audience persistently asked when I would write a book documenting the architecture and sculpture of Rice. In response to those many requests, interpreted as popular demand, I have enlarged the scope of the other presentations.

My primary purpose in developing this walking-tour guide is to make the readers who have visited the Rice campus, or who may even have lived here for four years or more, aware of the fascinating details in stone, metal, brick, or clay that they failed to notice during their stay. Publication costs do not permit me to make your tour a photographic documentary of the campus, but the written text will approach a documentary description of most of the buildings and items of interest.

Over the years I have also stumbled upon some intriguing anecdotes, a few of which I will share with you. Unfortunately, I cannot include some of the interesting stories about the university in this brief guide, but many of them are told in *A History of Rice University: The Institute Years, 1907–1963*, by Fredericka Meiners (Rice University Studies, 1982). I highly recommend that book to every former Rice student as interesting and fascinating reading. Another publication of must-read status is *Architecture at Rice: The General Plan of the William M. Rice Institute and Its Architectural Development*, Monograph 29 of the Architecture Department by Stephen Fox. One entire satellite saga that should someday be recorded is the story of Oswald J. Lassig, the sculptor who did virtually all the carving on campus through the time when Cohen House was built. The architectural detail from which the beauty of Rice derived could also in itself be the subject of a paper. Such Italian predecessors as the Doge's Palace in Venice, Giotto's campanile at the cathedral in Florence, and the other lovely campaniles throughout Italy were equaled in many ways by the work of the architects who created the Rice buildings.

I do anticipate that I will eventually write the story of Mr. Lassig, at which time I will seek assistance from a number of his descendants, native Texans who live in the Houston and Austin areas. Until then, we shall continue to enjoy his work and that of James Chillman, David Parsons, William McVey, and others through this book, but more by repeated visits to the campus. Photography is a wonderful medium, but there is absolutely no substitute for experiencing in person the actual buildings, spaces, and delightful details of the Rice University campus.

Many present and former faculty members and students have contributed to this publication. Where space has permitted, I have included the construction slides that Mr. Watkin gave me for use in my structures course in architecture. Through his talks before such groups as the Houston Philosophical Society, he also contributed valuable information about the development of the plans and design of the campus. Nolan E. Barrick, who received his B. A. degree in architecture in 1935 and is Professor Emeritus of Architecture at Texas Tech University, provided me with a copy of a letter from Dr. William N. Craig, formerly of the chemistry faculty at Rice. It was addressed to Mr. Watkin and explained many of the alchemical and chemical symbols that appear on the Chemistry Building. G. Holmes Richter, Professor Emeritus of Chemistry, pointed me in the direction of books on the history of chemistry located in Fondren Library. David G. Parsons, Professor Emeritus of Fine Arts, has been more than helpful in identifying his "bricks" on the Biology, Geology, and Space Sciences Buildings. On a number of occasions I used Mr. J. T. McCants' paper about the early days of Rice for verification of information. Others whom I consulted were Dr. Charles W. Philpott of biology, Dr. Kristine Wallace of classics, and, I'm afraid, those forgotten ones.

In conclusion, it is my hope that I can make the reader feel the beauty, delight, and even the humor of the Rice campus, and that he or she will be irresistibly stimulated to return and search for items that even I have failed to see.

Introduction

The architectural history of what we now call Rice University began in 1909 when Dr. Edgar Odell Lovett met with the firm of Cram, Goodhue and Ferguson of New York and Boston. From their meetings a general plan for the Rice Institute was developed. They considered and discarded a number of styles. The "collegiate Gothic" of West Point Military Academy and Princeton University, with its small windows and steep roofs, was quite inappropriate. At the time, relations with Mexico were hardly ideal, so a style similar to the Spanish Romanesque or the Mission style of Mexico was eliminated. At one point Mr. Cram prepared a sketch for Lovett Hall that, with round arched cloisters, twelve columns rising from twelve piers, open loggias, and Gothic niches, resembled St. Mark's in Venice. This design, however, did not even reach the discussion stage, as it was characterized by one observer as "wedding-cake" architecture. The discussants ultimately agreed that the style of the Institute should be appropriate to the climate of the region and should strive to represent the development of the Romanesque in Italy, had the beginning of Gothic not terminated the development of Romanesque.

The Boston and New York offices of the firm held an inhouse competition for the master plan. The Boston office under Cram developed a grand plan in which the academic court was almost a mile long; in the Goodhue plan of the New York office, the academic court was about one-half mile in length. In both cases, access to the buildings was from a point on Old Main Street Road further from the city of Houston than the present location of Gate Number 1 at Main Street and Sunset Boulevard—a rather serious mistake considering the condition of Old Main Street Road at the time. William Ward Watkin was assigned the task of combining the two plans and of including some of the recommendations of the trustees. The result was a plan in which the academic court was only a quarter mile in length (1,300 feet), and access was provided at the point on the 290 acres nearest the city of Houston. (See photograph 4.)

The design of the new university, which had neither faculty nor students and which was located almost two miles from the city limits, presented

xi

unusual problems, in that none of the usual city services were available. Power and water were immediate needs, and some provision for sewage disposal was obviously a must. Drainage of the site had to be provided as well, since no assistance could be anticipated from Harris County toward this end. The western one-third of the site was subject to regular overflowing of Harris Gully, although the balance of the site could hardly be characterized as arid at any time. The immediate needs of the new university were to be served by the construction of an Administration Building (renamed Lovett Hall in December 1947); the Mechanical Laboratory, the power plant with its stately smokestack, the campanile; a dining hall; and a dormitory (South Hall, now part of Will Rice College). The Administration Building housed the Library, the Faculty Chamber, a number of classrooms, and faculty and administrative offices. The Mechanical Laboratory housed engineering, architecture, and several other departments, with classrooms and laboratory facilities.

The adoption of Italian Romanesque as a style dictated a philosophy in the use of materials: those buildings located on the academic court were to be rich in marble and stone with small areas of brick. Academic buildings not on the academic court were to have less marble, but considerably more stone and brick, whereas the residential buildings were to be predominantly stucco with a limited use of stone and brick. This distribution of materials is still evident in Venice and elsewhere in Italy today.

Originally the Rice Institute was scheduled to open in 1911, but in keeping with the good intentions of the construction industry and the optimism of architects, the new university opened its doors in September 1912. Dr. Lovett's dream, as well as those dreams of the Board of Trustees, had been realized. And so Dr. Lovett occupied his new office, which was located on the fourth floor of the Administration Building directly over the Sallyport. Some years later, Dr. Hubert Bray of the Department of Mathematics represented Dr. Lovett on the occasion of the inauguration of the president of Texas A&M University. On that occasion he carried the greetings of the Rice Institute to the sister institution and wrote:

A great man is Edgar O. Lovett.
His office has nothing above it.
It is four stories high,
As high in the sky
As William Ward Watkin could shove it.

We will look at many of the wonderful features of Lovett Hall and the other campus buildings during our tour of the Rice University grounds. So put on your walking shoes, or relax in a comfortable chair, and join me at Gate Number 1.

A Walking Tour of **Rice University**

James C. Morehead, Jr.

Rice University Studies

Houston, Texas

Copyright © 1984 by Rice University

All rights reserved

Printed in the United States of America

Library of Congress Cataloging in Publication Data

Morehead, James C., 1913–
   A walking tour of Rice University

  (A Rice University Studies special publication)
   1. Rice University—Description—Views. 2. Rice University—Buildings—Pictorial works. 3. Rice University—Guide-books. I. Title. II. Series.
LD6053.M66   1984   378.764′1411
84-60486

ISBN 0-89263-256-9 clothbound
ISBN 0-89263-257-7 paperbound

2

3

4

5

6

7.

8.

9

10

11

12

13

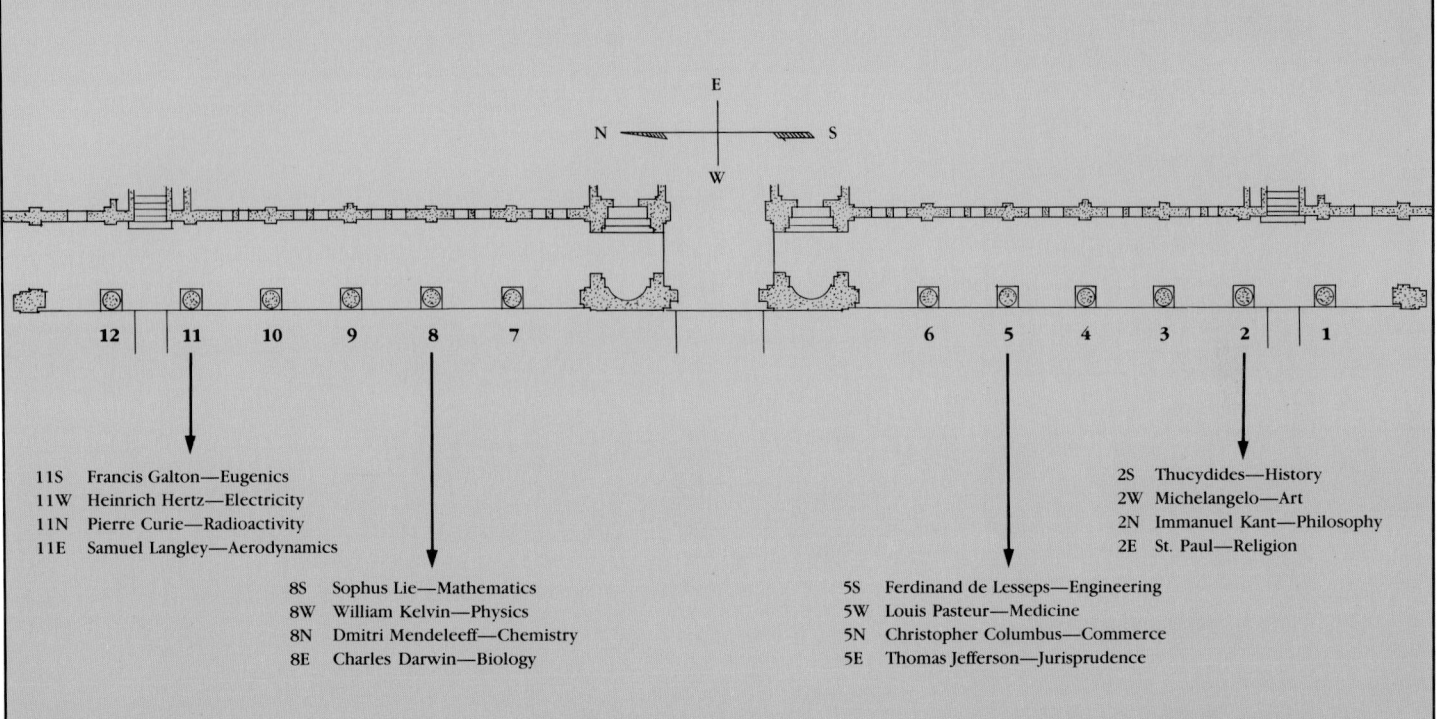

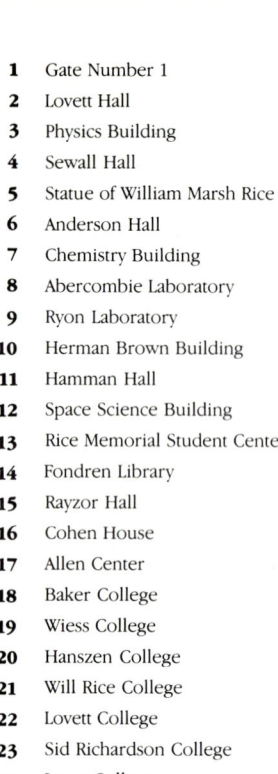

1 Gate Number 1
2 Lovett Hall
3 Physics Building
4 Sewall Hall
5 Statue of William Marsh Rice
6 Anderson Hall
7 Chemistry Building
8 Abercombie Laboratory
9 Ryon Laboratory
10 Herman Brown Building
11 Hamman Hall
12 Space Science Building
13 Rice Memorial Student Center
14 Fondren Library
15 Rayzor Hall
16 Cohen House
17 Allen Center
18 Baker College
19 Wiess College
20 Hanszen College
21 Will Rice College
22 Lovett College
23 Sid Richardson College
24 Jones College
25 Brown College
26 Keith-Wiess Geological Laboratories
27 Anderson Biological Laboratories
28 Rice Chapel

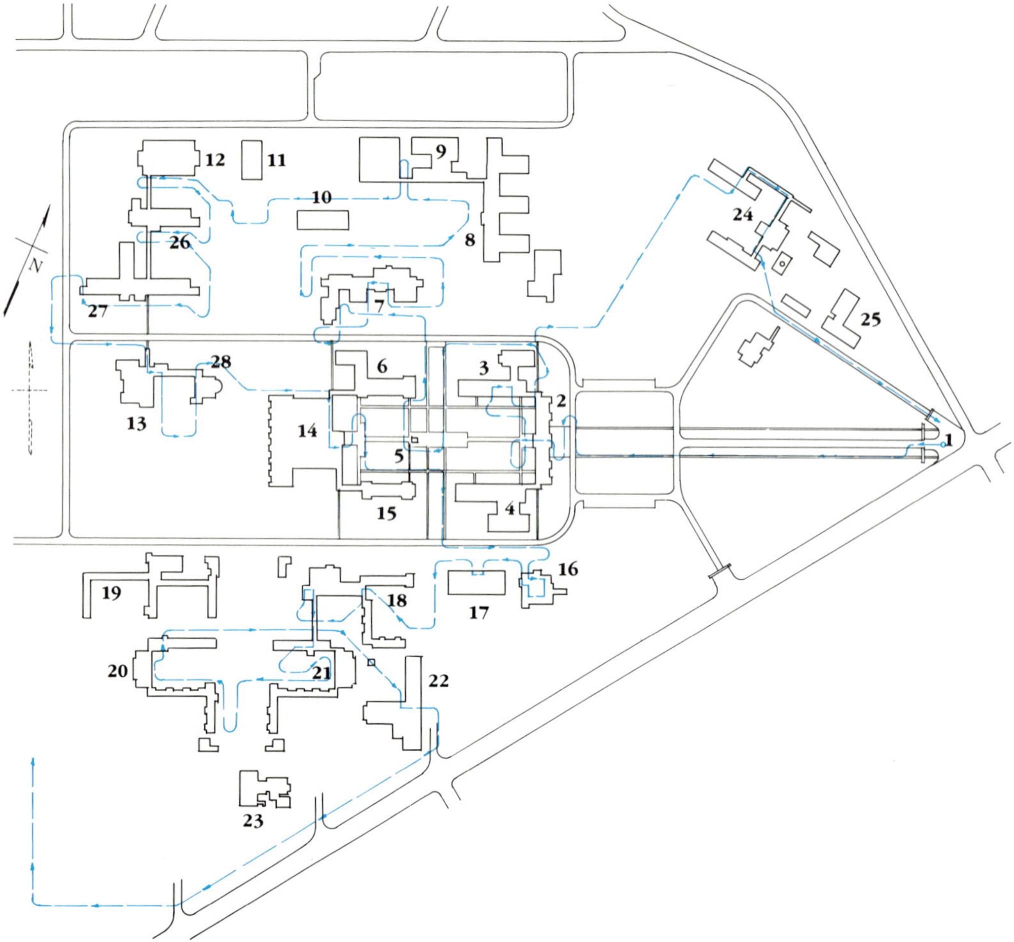

The Tour

Entrance

(See Color Plate 1.) We begin at Gate Number 1, at the corner of Main Street and Sunset Boulevard. Here the Rice University shield is placed on either side of the entrance. Gates 2 and 3 are similar in design, with a lantern but without the shields. Numerous Rice shields appear in and on buildings throughout the campus.

1
Look closely at the entrance piers at Gate Number 1, with their shields and wrought-iron lanterns. Until recently (1978) the brick and stone piers were covered with ivy.

From Gate Number 1, you may follow the diagram of the tour as shown. It will take real stamina to complete the full trip in just one session, but you can take such detours as suit your particular interests. You might want to scan the book quickly to determine which buildings and details you most want to see on your first walk.

2
This photograph shows the master plan of the campus as drawn by William Ward Watkin. The length of the academic court was reduced by one-half when Fondren Library was built in 1949. The library was originally intended to be located within the Graduate School complex at the north end of the cross axis beginning with Gate Number 4. That gate was to have been a main entrance to the campus, and it corresponded closely to the major access point of both the Boston plan and the New York plan of the architectural firm Cram, Goodhue and Ferguson. We will see this master plan again in bronze in the left hand of the founder, in the center of the academic court.

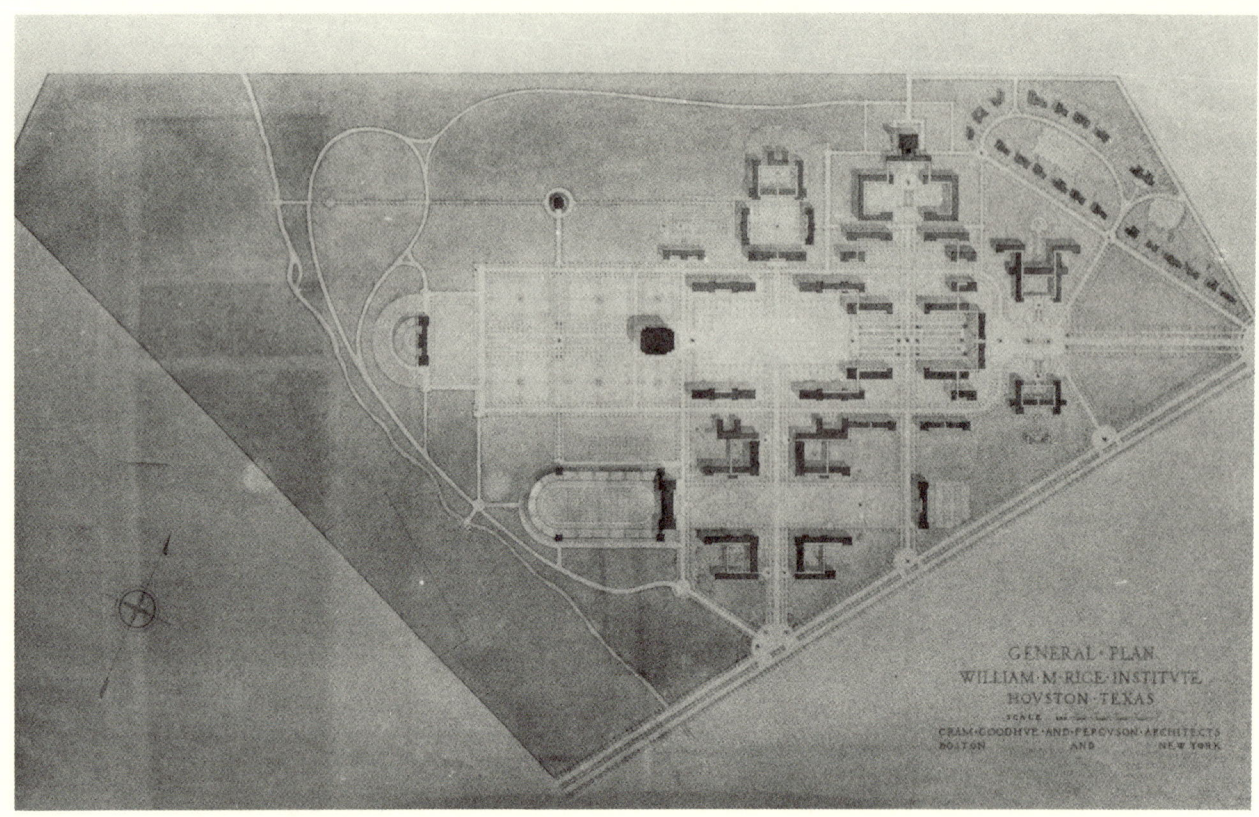

Another, more recent change in the original plan is the purchase in 1983 of the motor inn formerly known as the Tidelands, at the corner of South Main Street and University Boulevard, to be used as graduate-student apartments. For the first time since 1912, the campus has been extended beyond its original boundaries.

Lovett Hall

3
The Administration Building rises from the Texas prairie. The site could hardly have been called heavily wooded at the time, although now it is extremely difficult to photograph many campus buildings because of the trees. The original site was landscaped with trees provided by Teas Nursery.

(See Color Plate 2.) As we stroll from Gate Number 1 through a tree-lined walk, the Administration Building (now called Lovett Hall) bursts upon us. The rededication, when the building was renamed, is marked by an inscription on the south side of the Sallyport. I clearly recall doing the full-size drawing of the inscription for Mr. Watkin, reading: LOVETT HALL. IN GRATEFUL HOMAGE TO THE CLEAR VISION, UNFALTERING ZEAL AND BENEFICENT LABORS OF EDGAR ODELL LOVETT, FIRST PRESIDENT OF THE RICE INSTITUTE. EXEGIT MOMENTUM AERE PERENIUS. (The Latin is a quotation from Horace: "I have built a monument more lasting than bronze.")

(See Color Plate 3.) Approaching the building more closely, we could spend some time admiring the central tower. The beautiful Sallyport arch is flanked by long white applied columns that extend the full height of the building and are capped by lead-covered cupolas, the latter being particularly beautiful in themselves. Note the two handsome dark marble columns and the six smaller columns at the six pairs of windows. Dr. Lovett's office, as described in Dr. Bray's limerick, was located behind the upper three pairs. This central tower appears to be symmetrical, but you will surely spot the divergence from symmetry.

4
This photograph is a view of the Sallyport in the late afternoon. The changing sunlight enhances the beauty of the buildings as the shadows travel during the day. We will see other examples of this phenomenon later.

5
Three handsome bands of stone carving adorn the east side of the Sallyport. Two of them are floral in nature, and the third shows the column capital with the initial "R" and a delightful jester as part of the capital design. Above the capital on the band of carving is a pair of birds of questionable extraction, but possibly chaparrals.

6
Above the birds are a squirrel and several fish, with the pair of birds beginning a repetition of this threefold design.

(See Color Plate 4.) Flanking the Sallyport on each side are the two-story balconies with three monolithic white marble columns. Note the carved keystones in each arch and the colorful glazed tiles above.

7
Here, from an early construction slide, the white columns are being lifted into place. Fortunately, they didn't drop any of these!

8
And here is one of the stone keystones, another owl, a rather stylized one.

9
Some of the capitals are carved with a floral design, while others show the figure of a long-legged slender man emerging from the flower. These capitals were, of course, designed by the

architects in Boston, and it is rumored that the figure represented William Ward Watkin. I never heard either Mr. Watkin or Mr. Chillman confirm this, but the caricature is certainly in keeping with Mr. Watkin's physical "design." The white porcelain insulators on the corners of the capitals carry electrified wires intended to intimidate the many pigeons that try to nest on the campus buildings.

5

10
The cornerstone combines the shield of the State of Texas and another Rice Institute shield, and three are added to the growing family of owls. The Greek inscription translates: "'Rather,' said Democritus, 'would I discover the cause of one fact than become king of the Persians.'" Some have noted that this declaration was made at a time when to be king of the Persians was to rule the world. The Roman numeral indicating the date is interesting, because instead of MDCCCCXI it would normally be MCMXI. The latter is hardly as attractive architecturally.

11
If we look up as we pass through the Sallyport, we see the head of a senior with his mortar board. His face reflects the peace of accomplishment at having completed his degree requirements.

12
On the opposite side (north) is a very stern and worried head of the junior student, who still has those requirements to complete. His brow tells the story of his worries.

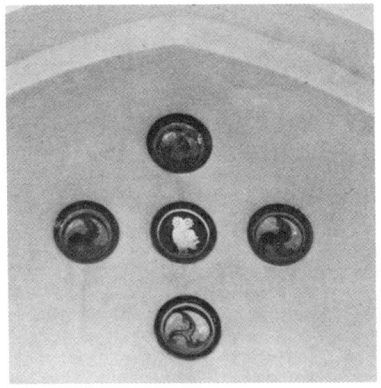

13
And on the west end of the Sallyport on the south side is the head of the all-knowing, all-seeing, and formerly immature freshman, the very mature sophomore.

14
Finally, opposite him, is the immature, giddy freshman, who is thrilled at having made it past the Admissions Committee, no doubt.

15
If you looked up as you passed through the Sallyport, you saw high on the south wall above the arches the circular ceramic of a little owl, with four circular ceramics each containing three dolphins. On the opposite wall, but not shown here, is a ceramic white star with the four ceramics of dolphins repeated. The original architect's drawings of these designs are on file in the Woodson Research Center of Fondren Library.

16
On the west side of Lovett Hall are twelve monolithic granite columns. Here is another actual construction photograph of one of these being lowered over a steel centering pin. This method of guaranteeing the exact location of the column on its base is hardly new. The Greeks used it, especially when columns were not monolithic and each section had to be located exactly in the center of the section below. However, they did not use steel centering pins, but lead or stone ones.

17
This, another construction photograph, is one of the twelve capitals on the granite columns. These were carved in place by Oswald J. Lassig, who immigrated to the United States from Germany in about 1905 and originally worked as a marble-cutter of tombstones in Chicago.

18
Mr. Lassig was brought to Houston in 1910 to do the carving on the Administration Building, and he became a Texan. He later owned and operated a limestone quarry in McNeil, Texas, just north of Austin; he and Mrs. Lassig raised their five children there. None of the five was born in the United States, though, since Mrs. Lassig always re-

turned to Germany when each child was to be born. Lassig was truly a remarkable artist, and he was commissioned to do work on later buildings on the campus, including the Chemistry Building and Cohen House. For his rich legacy of magnificent sculpture, he deserves to be included here. As I have said, the story of Mr. Lassig is one in itself and is too lengthy to be told here.

19
This is the west end of the Sallyport arch. The two bands of floral carving are similar to those on the east end. It should be noted, however, that all the carving on Lovett Hall was done in place.

20
But the other band is entirely different. It begins with a man with a ram, above which is a floral design. The first design at the bottom includes two seated figures that are not repeated again.

21
The carving of a peacock feeding is the next image, and then the floral pattern is repeated above that. These repeat alternately to the very top of the arch. Some have speculated whether there was any connection between the figure of the ram and the signs of the zodiac, or perhaps some other significance in the field of astronomy, since that was one of Dr. Lovett's fields of activity.

22
On the west facade of Lovett Hall, to the left (north) of the Sallyport, is a female figure holding an owl in her left hand. This is certainly Athena and her little owl, and this panel represents science. The inscription IF WE PROPERLY OBSERVE CELESTIAL PHENOMENA WE MAY DEMONSTRATE THE LAWS WHICH GOVERN THEM is a quotation from Aristotle and certainly refers to astronomy.

23
We can compare the bronze figure, "Athena Flying Her Owl," with her mirror image on Lovett Hall. Note that the bronze figure has the right knee slightly bent and is holding the owl in her right hand, whereas the stone figure has the left knee slightly bent and is holding the owl in her left hand, which is indeed a remarkable similarity. The only real difference is that

the bronze figure has her left arm raised, while the stone figure has her right arm on her head. The photograph of the bronze figure is reproduced through the courtesy of the Metropolitan Museum of Art, Harris Brisbane Dick Fund, 1950.

24
The female figure on the south side of the Sallyport represents the arts. LOVE, BEAUTY, JOY AND WORSHIP ARE FOREVER BUILDING, UNBUILDING AND REBUILDING IN EACH MAN'S SOUL is a quotation from Plotinus. When one of Lassig's children compared the face of the figure with a photograph of her mother, she was surprised to see that they were the same.

25
South of the Sallyport and above the arches are three carved plaques. The one on the left has the head of Homer on it and symbolizes letters. The inscription THE THING THAT ONE SAYS WELL GOES FORTH WITH A VOICE EVERLASTING is from the Greek poet Pindar.

26
The plaque in the center represents science and has the carved head of Isaac Newton. The quotation SPEAK TO THE EARTH AND IT SHALL TEACH THEE is from the biblical philosopher Job.

27
The plaque on the right with the head of Leonardo da Vinci represents art. Dr. Lovett himself wrote the accompanying inscription: THE CHIEF FUNCTION OF ART IS TO MAKE GENTLE THE LIFE OF THE WORLD. Dr. Lovett also composed the inscriptions on the cornerstones of all the buildings that were erected through 1916.

28
Again we are fortunate to have this construction slide of the west side of Lovett Hall showing the applied columns with their handsome capitals. The brickwork and stonework had not yet been set in place behind them. The pelican and the owl capitals are in the foreground. I hope you have noticed that there are innumerable birds of all sizes and shapes on the campus buildings.

29
A similar view of the completed building was taken from the roof of the cloister that connects Lovett Hall and Sewall Hall.

30
The owl capital is shown with the wise old bird on three sides of the capital. As noted above, you will see many other birds if you are observant, such as doves, peacocks, and chaparrals (road-runners).

31
Here are the pelicans on the tall applied columns. There are only two on each capital, since they are carved on the corners rather than on the faces of the capitals.

32
Now we see the capital with the seal of Aesculapius, the Roman god of medicine. On the preliminary campus plan prepared in Boston, provision was actually made for a medical school.

Now we return to the twelve granite columns that line the cloister on the west side of Lovett Hall, six on each side of the Sallyport. There are three types of capitals on them; each type occurs four times. (See Figure 2.)

33
Counting from the south (refer to Figure 2), columns 1, 4, 9, and 12 are the chaparral capitals. The chaparral is also a native Texan, and the fact that it is a member of the cuckoo family is, I'm sure, irrelevant.

34
Columns 3, 6, 7, and 10 are the campus life capitals, showing a coed with her 1912 mod hat, the intrigued student with an unread book in his lap looking her way, and the football player, also in a 1912 uniform and undoubtedly interested, as he is running in her direction. He has been chasing her unsuccessfully on these capitals since 1912!

35
Columns 2, 5, 8, and 11 are carved with the heads of the founders of various disciplines, or the leaders in various fields of endeavor. Referring again to the diagram, the persons whose heads are represented on columns 2, 8, and 11 are not shown here. Amazingly, two of the men represented were cousins: Charles Darwin and Sir Francis Galton were grandsons of Erasmus Darwin, the English naturalist and poet. Only those heads on column 5 are shown here, the first on the south side of the column being Ferdinand de Lesseps, a French diplomat and engineer who represents the field of engineering; he was honored for his part in constructing the Suez Canal.

36
On the west side of column 5 is Louis Pasteur, a French chemist and bacteriologist, representing medicine.

37
On the north side is Christopher Columbus, the Italian explorer and navigator, who represents commerce.

38
And on the east (cloister) side is Thomas Jefferson—statesman, lawyer, and architect—who represents jurisprudence.

These capitals bear a remarkable resemblance to those on the Doge's Palace in Venice. Those in Italy, however, are not as large as the Rice ones, nor are they nearly so finely carved. An article in the *Houston Post* at the time of the official opening of the new institute reported that some of the heads on the columns were being carved out of historical sequence, and that Mr. Watkin asked Mr. Lassig to attempt to change them by cutting the stone more deeply. Mr. Lassig is supposed to have been successful in doing so. The precise sequence of dates, though, seems to correlate only approximately with the men's sequence on the capitals. On the other hand, the same newspaper reported that the head on the north side of column 11 is that of James Currie, a Scottish physician, whereas all subsequent references are to Pierre Curie, the French scientist. In any case, none of these uncertainties detracts from the beauty of the capitals and the fascination they hold for us.

Much has been said about the brickwork on Lovett Hall. Because of the unusually thick bed of mortar of one inch, it was impossible to lay more than two or three courses of brick a day. It has also been said that this heavy mortar joint gave the brickwork a horizontal feeling; but that appearance, while true, is not due to the horizontal joint alone. The unsung trick lies in the almost total absence of mortar in the vertical head joint. An interesting exercise exists in comparing the appearance of the brickwork on Lovett Hall with that on the Ryon Engineering Laboratory. The existence of a considerable head joint on the latter building gives the brickwork quite a different effect.

39
On the cloisters connecting Lovett Hall to the Physics Building and Lovett Hall to Sewall Hall are five carved medallions and two carved shields. These are similar in feeling to some on the Giotto cathedral tower in Florence, Italy, although the latter are in a diamond shape instead of a circle. From

left to right, these are the shield of the State of Texas (not shown in the photograph); a man with a shovel, representing agriculture; a man with a sphere, representing geography; a man with a book, representing literature; a man observing lightning, representing meteorology; a man with a chisel, representing sculpture; and the shield of the Rice Institute, with even three more owls.

There are actually three sets of medallions on each side of each cloister, but the shields are reversed in order in the third set. Can you find the miniature owl between the man with the chisel and the shield on the right? The small black spot on the edge of meteorology is a piece of ball moss.

40
Between the sets of medallions are two peacocks worked into a circular design, with a lamp of oil or a basket of fruit in the center.

(See Color Plate 5.) Here is the west elevation of Lovett Hall as it is seen from the statue of the founder. The shadows of the turrets of Sewall Hall on the right add movement and variety. Also, in the late afternoon the ceramic tiles along the upper part of the building reflect almost like gems.

Physics Building

41

Leaving Lovett Hall, we proceed to the next building constructed on the academic court. The Physics Laboratory was built in 1914, and the architects were of course Cram, Goodhue and Ferguson. Although it is not obvious from this photograph, the arches are not all the same height, the tallest being located in the center under the stone balcony. The cornerstone on the southwest corner of the building continues the method of recording the date in Roman numerals: MDCCCCXIV. Thanks to the head stonemason, Mr. Ernest W. Harrowing, I am fortunate to have a 4" x 6" portion of a slab of dark green veined marble that was to have been placed on the south wall of the building near the west end. This piece of marble was rejected by Mr. Watkin, since it was slightly damaged.

(See Color Plate 6.) The main entrance to the Physics Building shows its brilliant mosaic designs.

42
A balcony over the main entrance serves as a pigeon rookery, which fortunately is not obvious from below. However, it does not make for a pleasant experience to get access to the balcony from one of the Physics lecture rooms to photograph the handsome owls.

43
On each corner of the balcony is a stone owl, and here is one of them. This is probably the finest carved owl on the entire campus. Even today the chisel marks on his feathers are distinct and unweathered.

44
A portion of the south facade shows the different heights of the arches and the handsome turrets. Under these turrets are a series of ventilating shafts that previously permitted fumes from the chemistry laboratories below to be exhausted into the atmosphere. While no longer used in that manner, a few

are used in connection with the air conditioning, which was installed at a later date. When chemistry moved to its own facilities in 1925, the pigeons promptly moved into the vents. They were later evicted.

45
There are a number of attractive drinking fountains around the campus, some, but not many, still being operational. You will find this one of marble and stone at the west end of the physics cloisters.

46
Just before entering the building, you will see two brick niches, one on each side. While these niches are attractive examples of fine brickwork with wedge-shaped bricks and bricks with curved surfaces, the students find

them amusing, as they are known as "whispering niches." If two people climb into the two niches and kneel with their backs to each other, the person in one niche can converse with the person in the other by speaking in a whisper. If you are young you might try it.

47
A particularly interesting angle shows the turrets on the rear of the building partially framed by those on the front. Shadows of the turrets on the Physics Amphitheatre are continually changing. At times the shadow of only one turret is seen, while at other times, both turrets cast shadows on the wall behind.

48
The architects even designed the hardware for the first buildings. The original drawings for this snake may be seen in the archives in Fondren Library, as may the drawing of the peacock door plates.

49
Notice the door plate designed with a pair of peacocks.

50
Inside the main entrance to the Physics Building is a lobby with a tiled, vaulted ceiling. Incorporated in the ceiling design are four special tiles with human figures on them and the words "Mind" (shown here), "Method," "Matter," and "Motion." This lobby is extremely alive acoustically, so if you stand in the center and clap your hands, the space will clap back at you.

51
At the high point of the ceiling is a ceramic tile star, I presume of the State of Texas.

23

52
In this same lobby there are four very handsome bronze owls that are part of the design of the original light fixtures. Early in the morning of April 15, 1983, all four of these were disconnected and stolen. This created quite a stir, as the university alerted antique dealers throughout the country to be on the alert for them; the press also reported their theft. Dr. Stephen Baker, a member of the physics faculty, offered a $500 reward for information leading to their recovery. Later Dr. Baker received an anonymous poem that, through interpretation of a riddle, led to their recovery and eventual reinstallation. Two of them were found on the roof of Lovett Hall, and the other pair in the basement of Lovett Hall near the Admissions Office files.

53
This cloister with particularly nice architectural detailing connects the main Physics Building to the Physics Amphitheatre. Another of the drinking fountains is located at the south end of this cloister. A construction photograph taken about 1913, which I could not include, shows this same view about half completed. Notice how much more brick there is on the Amphitheatre, it not being located directly on the academic quadrangle. Note also the handsome shadows of the turrets on the Physics Building. These shadows move from west to east every day of the year, the vertical location of the shadows depending on the time of day and the time of year.

54
Look closely at the east end of the Amphitheatre; shown here is the center of three sets of three windows each, and the pairs of delicate marble columns between the windows.

55
Over the north entry to the Amphitheatre is a carved stone pediment with even another Rice shield. The floral pattern contains at least one bird of doubtful ancestry. The carving over this entrance and on each side is stonework that goes unnoticed by most people but is extremely interesting. (See Color Plate 7.) This is a detail of one of the two stone owls on the Amphitheatre and the multicolored mosaic design around the inlay of black marble.

56
On each side of this entrance are two carved panels that are especially delightful. In the top panel the student with a book at one end and the ancient professor or philosopher at the other are probably clear in their meaning, but the bottom panel is not so obvious. It is believed that the bird and the peccary (javelina) represent the animals on Noah's Ark, but I would have thought they should appear in pairs. The central figure may be Adam in the

Garden of Eden, with the sun causing luxuriant growth in the garden. The two figures on the other end may indeed be Cain and Abel. Each figure holds a weapon of some sort in his hand; but Cain, who appears to have the upper hand, surprisingly wears what appears to be a coonskin cap! The biblical interpretation is a nice one, it being very hard to relate these carvings directly to the field of physics.

At this point you might wish to digress from the tour to cross the road and strike out in the direction of Jones and Brown Colleges, since this is our nearest point to them. (In that case, refer to photographs 199–201.) I prefer to make a separate visit at the end, since they can then be visited with the other colleges.

Sewall Hall

57
The east end of the academic court was completed with the construction of Cleveland Sewall Hall in 1971. The architects, Lloyd and Jones, admirably solved the problem of providing a building that conforms to the original campus plan and resembles the building on the opposite side of the academic court, yet serves functions entirely different from those of the Physics Building. The donor, Mrs. Cleveland Sewall, provided sufficient funds that the turrets and much of the carving on the Physics Building could be reproduced. Also, although not identical, the arches, fenestration, and com-

bination of marble, stone, and brick almost match the other building. However, there is no balcony with marvelous stone owls, and this is natural since the main entrance is not located at the highest of the arches. On a number of places on the roof, glass roofing tiles were used in place of the clay tiles to permit natural light to enter the fine arts studios below.

58
This interesting view of the juncture of Lovett Hall and Sewall Hall seems to indicate that there is a stairway to the roof of the connecting cloister, but this is just another of the many variations of shadows that add interest to the campus.

Academic Court

59
In the center of the academic court is the statue of the man who made it all possible: William Marsh Rice. It is also his tomb. This monument was executed by the sculptor John Angell in 1930.

60
On the east side of the monument is the seal of Rice Institute with the inscription SALVE AETURNUM AETERNUMQUE SALVE. This is a quotation from Virgil, but Latin scholars report that it was a salutation used in Roman funerals, where the free translation became "Farewell forever and forever, farewell." Literally translated, the inscription reads "Hail forever and forever, hail." The south side of the pedestal has the seal of the State of Massachusetts, where Mr. Rice was born. The quotation is translated, "By the sword we seek peace, but peace only under liberty." On the west face under the shield of the United States is the familiar Latin phrase E PLURIBUS UNUM: "From many one." And on the north side of the pedestal is the seal of the State of Texas with the inscription IMPERIUM IN IMPERIO. This quotation translated is "empire within an empire" and is borrowed from the motto of the State of Ohio.

61

In the left hand of the founder on a bronze scroll is the master plan of the university. This can be viewed on tiptoe by basketball players, but the rest of us need some mechanical aid. It is very easy to recognize the locations of many of the buildings on campus, including Lovett Hall, the Physics Building, Sewall Hall, Anderson Hall, Rayzor Hall, and others. You won't find the library on this master plan. But compare it with photograph 2 to recognize the similarities as well as the variances from the original plan.

62

On the back of Mr. Rice's chair is the shield of the university repeated again, this time in bronze. The three owls on this shield are different from any others on the various Rice shields—much more lifelike with the very large left eye, the right eye being barely visible. Few people are aware of the location of this shield and these unusual owls.

Anderson Hall

63

Anderson Hall's contribution to the architectural interest of the campus is a bit limited, but one thing that the students really enjoy is the decorative frieze cut into marble at the entry nearest the statue. If you run your finger rapidly over the vertical row of holes, a derisive sound very similar to the "Bronx cheer" is generated. Perhaps this was an effort on the part of the architect to achieve sound in architecture. Try it and you'll try it more than once!

When Anderson Hall was built in 1947, the architects were Staub, Rather and Howze. Major additions and alterations were made in 1981 when James Sterling was the architect, with McEnany and Ambrose being the local representatives for Mr. Sterling. (McEnany is the son of the late Michael V. McEnany, who was professor of electrical engineering, registrar, and dean of undergrduate affairs for many years.)

When the building was remodeled, a feature somewhat reminiscent of the turrets on the Physics Building and on Sewall Hall was introduced. These were the "lanterns," but their function is entirely different, since their purpose is to admit light into the interior.

Chemistry Building

64

The Chemistry Building was built in 1925, with William Ward Watkin, Cram and Ferguson as associated architects. It is a storehouse of symbols, some of which date back to the Chaldean civilization of 1500 B.C. and beyond. At least two volumes explaining the details are available in Fondren Library for those who wish to delve more deeply into the various symbols. This photograph, taken around 1930, shows the rose garden of the legendary Tony Martino (master of campus planting), where Anderson Hall is now located. It is no longer possible to photograph this building because of the planting obscuring it.

65
Notice the arched entrance to the cloister at the lower entry to the Chemistry Lecture Hall. The arch was located too far to the left during construction, there being no brick between the stone on the left side of the opening and wall of the lecture hall, while there are ten inches of brick or more between the stone on the right of the opening and the brick pier. Had the arch been moved five inches to the right, there would have been space for all three fates on the left capital.

66
I photographed a print of the original tracing of the three fates of destiny from Greek mythology, where Clotho spins the thread of life, Lachesis measures it, and Atropos severs it. Our three fates of academic destiny are Samuel Glenn McCann, the director of admissions; Harry Caldwell, dean of the Institute, who is measuring (by grades) the thread of knowledge; and Dr. Radoslav Tsanoff, chairman of the Committee on Examinations and Standings, who severs the academic thread with a menacing pair of shears. The original drawings of the other three capitals are in the university archives, but the original drawing of the three fates has been lost. Fortunately a print was made before it disappeared. These four capital designs were made by James Chillman of the faculty in architecture.

67
Only Mr. McCann and Dean Caldwell made it in the final carving.

68
On the opposite side of the arch is a freshman in Chemistry 100 with his bunsen burner, extracting poison from the dragon's tooth.

69
Around the corner is the carving of the tall (6 foot, 4 inch), thin (140 pounds), very lengthy-legged William Ward Watkin with a T-square in hand. Architectural students are bowing down in due respect, perhaps to the Lord High Executioner, and Mr. Watkin has one foot on the neck of a freshman. Mr. Chillman's original pencil drawing showed a halo over Mr. Watkin's head, but this was deleted by the architect. (Architecture was housed in this building when it was completed.)

70
The last capital is a huge winged dragon with the head of Harry B. Weiser, instead of the usual crested head. Note the terrible claws with which the dragon subdues a student. The head in the upper right-hand corner is that of Mr. Flanigan, who was in charge of the chemistry storeroom and was Dr. Weiser's good and faithful assistant.

71
You will want particularly to appreciate the impressive upper entrance to the Chemistry Lecture Hall.

72
Now we see a circular design called an *enigma*, this being Kircher's enigma. These were designed by the alchemists to confuse the observer and were intended to conceal what was considered a basic principle of alchemy. A drawing of this may be found in the book *A History of Chemistry from the Earliest Times*, by James Campbell Brown (Philadelphia: P. Blakiston's Son & Co., 2nd ed., 1920). The first letter of each word in the outer ring spells SVLPHVR (sulphur); in the middle ring, FIXVM; and in the inner ring, EST SOL. Combining these into a single sentence, we get SULPHUR FIXUM EST SOL. The word *sol* is translated "gold," since gold was symbolized by the sun. The expression then reads, "Fixed sulphur is synonymous with gold."

73
On the face of the chemistry tower is Basil Valentine's enigma. In this case the first letters of the words spell "vitriol." The seven circular forms at the top are the symbols of the seven metals; the eagle is symbolic of the volatile (unstable) principle and the lion of the fixed (stable) principle.

74
On each side of the chemistry tower are entrances to the building with pairs of white columns supporting three stone arches. This cloister creates an outside vestibule where several stone carvings of a pair of dragons are located. The one with wings represents mercury—the volatile principle and the female—while the one without wings represents sulphur—the fixed principle and the male. (There was no pretense of equality between the sexes in those days.) For many years the annual commencement was held under a tent located in the court created by the

tower, these entrances, and the two adjacent laboratory wings. Don't fail to look up to the third floor on each side of the tower to enjoy the delicate little pink columns and supported arches.

75

On the cloister to the right of the tower are two triangular symbols in stone. These are equilateral triangles with the vertices down, the one on the left signifying water and the one on the right with a horizontal bar representing earth. On the left of the tower are two similar stone triangles, but with the vertices of the triangles up. The one on the left is fire, and the one on the right with a horizontal crossbar is air. The latter pair are badly weathered and should be replaced.

76
The chemistry tower itself is the location of a number of interesting symbols; in particular, the first part of the periodic table is recorded in contemporary symbols on the octagonal portion of the tower.

77
In 1869 Mendeleeff, whose head you may recall appears on the north side of column 8 on Lovett Hall, first organized the periodic table, in which he arranged the elements in order of their atomic weights. The lightest element shown on the tower is helium (He), followed in order by lithium (Li), beryllium (Be), boron (B), carbon (C), nitrogen (N), oxygen (O), and fluorine (F). In this photograph we see helium and lithium.

78
Identification of many of the symbols on the Chemistry Building was made much easier by a letter written to William Ward Watkin by Dr. William N. Craig, a member of the chemistry faculty in 1923. Of the many symbols that he describes or sketches, one is the symbol for phlogiston, a theory of combustibility supported by some chemists between 1650 and 1775. The same symbol is also shown in the circular ceramic tiles in some of the arched windows. The principle was that every material that was flammable contained some property within it that caused it to burn. Of course, there was also a group of chemists called antiphlogistics. This symbol appears on four sides of the tower just below the level where it changes from a square to an octagon.

37

79
The east and west ends of the Chemistry Building have been obscured by the recent addition of stair towers, but some of the symbols in glazed tile were included in the additions. They were occasionally installed upside down or sideways. The original east end was particularly attractive, with a stone balcony over the entrance door, pairs of windows with a marble column in the center at the second- and third-floor levels, and three little arches at the attic level. The balcony over the entrance was relocated over the new entrance, but it was a shame to lose the delicate windows and columns! In the court adjacent to the Chemistry Lecture Hall is another stone balcony that is somewhat similar to the original one at the east end. In this court we also see the marble columns at the third-floor level, which are a continuation of those on each side of the chemistry tower.

80
Many of the circular ceramic symbols located in the arches of the Chemistry Building are identified in James Campbell Brown's book, cited earlier. I like to think of these as the della Robbias of the Rice campus, as they are quite similar to the real thing in Italy. This is the symbol for gold, represented by the sun. They may have thought the sun was a planet.

81
And here we see the symbol for copper, also representing the planet Venus. One writer feels that this symbol represents Venus's hand mirror. It actually goes back many centuries to the Chaldeans, whose "chemists" associated the "seven" metals with the seven planets that they knew. If you see this symbol installed upside down (I couldn't find one), it is the symbol for antimony and not upside down at all. If you find it sideways, which it is on at least one occasion, it represents the license of the brickmason.

82
This symbol for iron, representing also the planet Mars, has become very popular today. But remember that the symbol dates back many centuries. Again, this is reported to represent the shield and spear of Mars, the god of war.

83
Also representing the planet Jupiter is the symbol for tin.

84
Here is lead, representing the planet Saturn.

85
Then silver, represented by the Moon.

86
And mercury, obviously representing the planet Mercury.

87
In the book *Chemie et Chemistes* by R. Massain, which is written mostly in French, this symbol is for water, composed of one atom of hydrogen (on the left) and one atom of oxygen (on the right). At least that's the way they thought it was! John Dalton, an English chemist, thought of the atoms as being spherical; hence so many of the symbols are indicated with various combinations of circles.

88
And here is the symbol for ammonia, composed of one atom of nitrogen and one of hydrogen.

89
This is the symbol for oxynitric acid.

90
This symbol is incorporated into the building upside down on at least one occasion and represents volatile alkali.

91
This is fixed alkali.

92
And here is sulphuric acid.

93
This is nitric acid. I'm not sure what the difference is between oxynitric acid and nitric acid, but there are different symbols for them.

94
Finally, this is hydrochloric acid. I'm sure I must have missed at least one symbol, but the books to which I have referred should show them all. Do not fail to walk around to the north and west sides of the Chemistry Building. Many of the alchemical symbols are on the north side, and it especially is rich in other architectural detail as well.

Abercrombie Engineering Laboratory

95
From the Chemistry Building we move on to the J. S. Abercrombie Laboratory for electrical engineering, built in 1948, also the work of Staub, Rather and Howze. This was the second project in a rash of construction that began in 1947 with Anderson Hall and ended with Fondren Library in 1949. This building did hold rather closely to the philosophy that academic buildings off the main academic court should be built with more stone and brick and less marble.

96

The only ornamentation on the building is the stone carving by William McVey. This figure represents man taking energy from the heavens (the sun) and putting it to work on the earth. The building and the sculpture are difficult to photograph because of the many Japanese rain trees. An enormous area of the second floor was the location of an equally enormous computer, the first built on the Rice campus.

97

From some earlier day, in the 1930s or 1940s, comes this lovely but unusual photograph of the campus. Notice the very unattractive parking lots in front of the Administration Building and the old Mechanical Laboratory! What an improvement today's arrangement is. If you thought back to the construction dates of Anderson Hall and Fondren Library you might be a bit confused, because Fondren opened in 1949, whereas the J. S. Abercrombie Laboratory was completed in 1948 and doesn't show at all! Closer examination of Anderson and Fondren will show that the east end of Anderson isn't at all as shown, nor are the arches and cloisters of Fondren as actually built. I suspect that photographs of the models of these two buildings were imposed upon the earlier photograph by the architects Staub, Rather and Howze to show the Board of Trustees how the new buildings would fit in.

Mechanical Laboratory

98
Moving back over the years, we have this construction photograph of the campanile tower as it was originally built in 1912.

43

(See Color Plate 8.) While you can't see the original on the tour, you can see it as remodeled in 1930 after it was struck by lightning. I personally think it is much more photogenic now.

99
This is a rather unusual view of the campanile, sometimes called a toad's-eye view. As you know, campaniles were originally bell towers, but ours is one of the most beautiful smokestacks ever built, and now nonpolluting, too.

100
While in the area of the original Mechanical Lab, you should enjoy the stone balcony with its seven ceramic symbols under the eave of the building. These ceramics are not as easy to see in the photograph as they are on the site, but the one in the middle is (surprise) an owl. Similar designs are under the eaves of the Physics Building.

101
And this inscription at the base of the column near the entrance looks very much like a contemporary logo: WMRI 1911.

102
Here on the north side of the Mechanical Lab, in at least two locations, is a blue ceramic shield flanked on each side by blue ceramic stars. It takes a little hunting to find these.

There is a very attractive brick niche on the south side of the building that is almost identical to the whispering niches at the Physics Building. This one, however, houses an inactive foun-

44

tain and is not a sound chamber. At one time an inscription in chalk on this brick niche read "fountain of youth."

Ryon Engineering Laboratory

103
Ryon Laboratory gives us another chance to see the campanile. This civil engineering building was financed mainly by the gift of Mr. and Mrs. L. B. Ryon, whose photograph hangs in the first-floor lobby. Mr. Ryon was chairman of that department for many years. When the Ryons' gift was announced, the remainder of the faculty was quick to remind the administration that the Ryons had not accumulated the funds from his Rice salary. This building was completed in 1965. Calhoun, Jackson and Dill were the architects.

Herman Brown Building

104
This is an interesting view of the Herman Brown Building, temporary home of the Jones School of Administration and, at the time the picture was taken, the Institute for Computer Services and Applications. (The computer center recently moved to the Mudd Building nearby.) Although the Herman Brown Building was constructed in 1968, it was not dedicated until 1971. The architects were George and Abel Pierce.

Hamman Hall

105
Next-door Hamman Hall, an auditorium with a capacity of about five hundred, is the home of the Rice Players and parts of the Shepherd School of Music. This building has many small glazed tiles, sometimes called "goodies," intermingled in the brickwork. The outside lobby of the building, like the entrance vestibule of the Physics Building, has a very high reverberation time. The inside lobby is also highly sound-reflective. A little hand-clapping here is both impressive and fun. Hamman Hall was officially opened in 1958 with the faculty Gilbert and Sullivan operetta *Princess Ida*. The selection was a particularly appropriate one, since this was also the first full year that Mary Gibbs Jones College was open. (The operetta is about a most unusual women's university.)

Space Science Building

106
From here we move to three science buildings, all of which were designed in the same architectural feeling by the same architects, Pierce and Pierce, who also designed Hamman Hall. The Space Science Building is the first of these, although it was actually built last, in 1966. Professor Emeritus David G. Parsons was commissioned to design special bricks for these buildings, and he carved a fascinating series of wood molds from which the sculptural bricks were cast. The story of the casting of these is one in itself, since a large majority of those manufactured had to be rejected. These bricks relate to the discipline of each building: space sciences, geology, and biology. Unlike the geology and biology buildings, this one did not have a special piece of sculpture in the stair tower on the east end. I understand the government paid for a large part of this building, so we were very lucky to be able to include even Mr. Parsons' bricks.

107
The symbol of gravity, an apple, of course.

108
Here is Saturn with its rings.

109
Now Sputnik, which was really responsible for launching the space program, including this building.

110
This (probably) is Halley's Comet. Not shown is a modern rocket superimposed on the first rocket, the Goddard Rocket. Others not shown are the Sun of Archimedes, the Aurora Borealis, disk antennae, spiral nebulae, an atomic particle, a proton, a neutron, and a symbol of the earth's magnetic fields.

Keith-Wiess Geological Laboratories

111
Now we come to the geology building, built in 1958. At one time there was a handsome and fascinating mobile in the stairwell at the east end. It was hung from the third-floor ceiling on a large swivel; but the high winds of Hurricane Carla caused it to break loose, and it was badly damaged. Dave Parsons was the designer and constructed it himself. It represented the galaxy of which our solar system is a part. The earth was a pretty small part of the system, but it was a delight to watch the metal and heavy stained glass parts revolve.

112
Here are a few of the bricks that relate to the field of geology. First is the chambered nautilus.

113
Then the fossil leaf.

114
And the trilobite.

115
Here is a seismograph reading. Other bricks that are not shown are two different representations of twin calcite crystals, the world symbol, earth strata, ammonite suture pattern, fossil bark, and the light interference pattern in crystals.

Anderson Biological Laboratories

116
Here we see the Biology Lecture Hall, a later addition to the group, and the open court between biology on the left and geology on the right.

When the biology building was originally constructed, a small horizontal slot was cut in one of the green marble panels on the north side. Through this slot hundreds of honeybees moved in and out from their hive inside the building. The queen and some of the bees had been brought from the Physics Building in 1958. It was a fascinating experience to search for the queen, who lived under glass so that the hive could be monitored. Alas, this prolific lady and her family no longer exist.

117
And here is a good photo of one of Dave Parsons' bricks, the moth.

119
Then the scorpion, one of my favorites.

118
Now the jellyfish.

120
And the molecular model of the amino acid glycine. You should search for a number of others: the squid, the starfish, the human embryo, a tapeworm, Wisconsin earthworms, hookworms, protozoa, cell division, the powerhouse of the cell (mitochondrion), and finally DNA.

121
The biology building, also built in 1958, is another of those buildings that is much obscured by landscaping. Hence the photograph of this building is of the west end, which is a more recent addition. In the east stairwell, however, is a three-story sculpture by Dave Parsons. The later addition to the west end obscured or covered up one of my favorite mistakes, a jellyfish brick incorporated into the masonry with the tentacles sticking up!

Rice Memorial Student Center and Chapel

122
Across the road we can see the handsome bronze push plates on the entrance to the Rice Memorial Center, showing a very nice R. I. above and a stylized owl below. When we enter the student center we are in the home of Sammy's (a cafeteria), the Campus Store, the Rice radio station KTRU, and Willie's Pub, the last being a favorite meeting spot for students and faculty. Alumni and student offices are also located here. On the original campus plan, this building was to be placed just east of the present location of Lovett College. Several other sites were proposed for it before it found a permanent home in 1958. Harvin Moore was the architect for both the Rice Chapel and the Rice Memorial Center.

123
Here is the campanile of the Memorial Center, and it is indeed a bell tower this time, albeit an electronic bell.

124
From this point near the Memorial Center one can look through the cloister of the Rice Chapel, through Anderson Biological Laboratories and Keith-Wiess Geological Laboratories, all the way to the Space Science Building.

125
These owl capitals near the chapel are almost identical to those on the south and north ends of the Lovett Hall cloisters.

126
The court between the grand ballroom of the Memorial Center and the chapel is a peaceful place to sit and have lunch, except when the Shepherd School of Music has an ensemble of some kind playing there. Their occasional programs, though, are a great addition. Many students and alumni are married in the chapel, a gift of Mr. and Mrs. J. Newton Rayzor. The Robert H. Ray court is often used for receptions and other ceremonies. Naturally, the pigeons have found this quiet spot and often raise families over the chapel entrance. Around the court are blue ceramic owls and the initials R. I. These circular ceramics also appear on the exterior of the circular apse of the chapel, as we shall see.

127
The "della Robbia" owl and "R. I." are much more visible in this enlargement.

(See Color Plate 9.) Here is the interior of the apse, with its brilliant gold mosaics.

(See Color Plate 10.) These are some of the stained-glass windows that admit rich colored light into the interior.

128
The university seal appears again on each end of the wood pews.

129
Adjacent to the chapel is a small meditation chapel. The ornaments on the altar are the work of Ruth Laird. It is well worth asking for the key to see this miniature gem of a space.

Fondren Library

130
From the chapel, we move to Fondren Library, walking through the cloisters and out in front of the building. You will see two large terra-cotta owls, which I find somewhat overweight and unattractive.

131
Fondren Library was completed in 1949 under architects Staub, Rather and Howze. Its location was the first real deviation from the original master plan, and that change forever defined the academic court as a much smaller space than on the original plan. Any future academic expansion will undoubtedly create secondary or tertiary academic courts.

The history of the development of writing is depicted in stone above the main entrance. There are a total of five carvings, and the first shows the earliest form of recording information—pictographic writing—with symbols of the civilizations who used this form of writing. Apparently even Noah used it, for closer examination of the lower right corner shows the ark.

132
On the next panel, cuneiform symbols are shown; these had their origin in Persia and Assyria. Some of the early tablets were found in Chaldea. The tablets, made of some of the earliest-used metals—gold, silver, copper, lead, and tin—contained the story of the construction of the palace in cuneiform. Syrian and Persian figures are shown, but one of the most interesting forms is the hard-to-recognize Chaldean ramped temple in the upper left-hand corner. Of course, cuneiform writing was used in Babylon, where the tower of Babel was built. When God realized that the people were trying to build a temple to heaven, he turned them all into foreigners and they went off to Europe and have been there ever since (with apologies to Roark Bradford).

133
Next we have some of the hieroglyphics of Egypt, with the Sphinx and the pyramid in the upper left-hand corner, and with the first paper, a piece of papyrus. We also see a part of the Greek alphabet, from which the Roman was derived, and Romulus and Remus being nursed by the wolf, and the Ionic column and the cross symbolizing the beginning of Christianity.

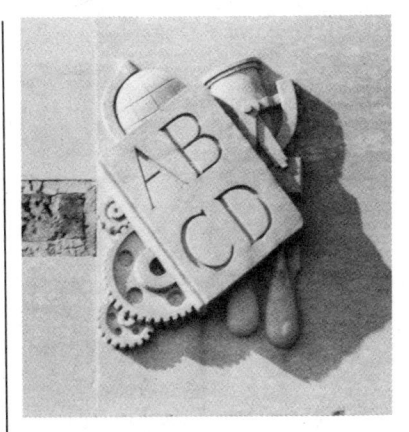

134
For some reason, hardly chronological, the next panel represents the industrial age and the mass production of books, including best sellers and paperbacks, no doubt. Some of the related symbols include the sphere of the world and the gears of the printing machines.

135
Just around the corner and apparently out of sequence is a panel that represents the era when books were copied by hand by monks in monasteries; the cross and the crusades represent Christianity and the knights with their maces in battle.

Rayzor Hall

Rayzor Hall is hardly a storehouse of architectural delight, but take note of the two shields over the south and north entrances. The first is the usual Rice shield; and the second, which is also in stone, is a shield representing various areas of the arts. A shield that is almost identical to the latter may be found on Hanszen College and will be shown later. The one on Hanszen differs in that it is a ceramic shield and has the word *Arts* under it. Staub, Rather and Howze were the architects for this building in 1962.

Cohen House

136
Our next stop is the Robert and Agnes Cohen House, the Faculty Club. Arriving at the structure, we stop to see the sundial, another gift of Mr. and Mrs. George Cohen. Cohen House was the first of the gifts to the university from the Cohens, this one being in honor of his parents. Mr. Cohen financed the building through a loan from the Rice Institute, which was a very nice arrangement for the Institute. He was subjected to much good-natured teasing over the years about obeying the one commandment (the fifth) that offered any reward. This building was constructed in 1927, and William Ward Watkin was the architect.

137
This photograph was taken of the paved terrace and cloister on the south side of the building before it was obscured by planting and before a later enlargement of the dining room. A small tiled fountain in the center of the terrace was enclosed by brick and stone piers, with wrought-iron fencing between some of the piers. With the exception of the fountain, this terrace was left in place when the size of the club was increased. One of the faculty picked up a piece of the tile when the fountain was being demolished, and that tile found its way into my hands, and eventually into the archives. The fountain, complete with water bubbling out of a pipe, created real problems for faculty mothers at the annual Easter egg hunt, as the little ones were naturally attracted to it and almost all tried to climb in at one time or another.

138
Here is another early view of the cloister where the heads of a number of the earlier faculty were cut in stone. The head of Asa Chandler of biology is on the column nearest the camera.

139
On the west side of the building is this very interesting entry to the club. The columns are reminiscent of some at St. Abbondio, a church in Como, Italy.

140
Here you can see the ornamental balcony with Italian Romanesque detail and the Rice shield, with the crest of the Cohen family, over the window.

141
Now we may enter the club through the original main entrance. While some, especially visitors, now come to the club by way of the new covered canopy at the east side of the new dining room, people arriving on foot from various parts of the campus are well rewarded for their walk.

142
Inside the club, passing through the lounge with its richly decorated ceiling, we come to the original stone cloister seen earlier. There we should note sculptures of the heads of Esther and George Cohen. Sculptured likenesses of the heads of his parents are also located here. These were added at about the time the new dining room was added in 1958 by Lloyd and Jones, Architects. Even I had a minor part in the construction of the club, for I made some changes in the second floor years ago, before the new dining room was added. In my experience, Mr. Cohen was a good client.

143
I cannot include photographs of all the heads of the faculty located in the club, such as Dr. Max Freund, formerly of the German department, who I think holds the Rice record for longevity—just over 100 years. The pair of Joe H. Pound of engineering and Herbert K. Humphrey of electrical engineering have also been omitted, but here is Harold A. Wilson of physics.

144
Since the name of each faculty member is on a small metal plate just below the head shown, it is easy for the tourist to identify them. Dr. Harry B. Weiser of chemistry is not shown here, but the head of William Ward Watkin is an excellent likeness.

145
I must include the head of Dr. Radoslav A. Tsanoff of philosophy. He was appointed a Distinguished Professor of Philosophy after he was supposed to retire, an arrangement by the Board of Trustees that allowed students to continue to experience his courses. The board made a total of five such appointments, as you will see. Dr. Tsanoff's daughter Katherine T. Brown is currently on the faculty in fine arts and for many years was dean of undergraduate affairs. Unfortunately, because of space limitations I cannot show a photograph of the head of Dr. Marcel Moraud of the French department, but you will see it on the wall.

146
Of international stature is Stockton Axson of the English department. Since Robert G. Caldwell of history was shown on the Chemistry Building, his photo is not included here. Others whom I am listing but not showing are the pair of Leon B. Ryon and H. Willis Slaughter, of civil engineering and sociology respectively, and Griffith Evans of mathematics.

147
It would never do to omit the pair of heads of John T. McCants and Samuel Glenn McCann, for they were a part of the lives of students almost from the beginning. Mr. McCann was the director of admissions (Admissions Committee, in fact) and registrar, and Mr. McCants was the bursar and on the faculty in English. He had originally come to Rice as Dr. Lovett's secretary in 1910. The two were often referred to as the positive and negative of the Rice Institute. Mr. McCann let you in and Mr. McCants often let you out, if you were in arrears with your bills.

148
When the new dining room was added to the Faculty Club, along with the enlarging of the kitchen facilities, the fountain that George Cohen had brought from Europe was incorporated into the design and was made a part of the walled garden. Without Mr. Cohen's knowledge, the Spanish moss that hung in profusion from the live oaks within the garden was removed. Mr. Cohen was both disappointed and disturbed by this and had more moss purchased and hung from the trees. Unfortunately, much of the new moss died. In connection with the addition, the financial arrangements were handled in the same way as for the original building, i.e., by obtaining a loan from Rice University and protecting that loan with a life insurance policy.

In the new dining room were two blank walls, on the east and west ends. Bill McVey was commissioned to use these walls for permanently recognizing more recent members of the faculty, a total of eighteen. These are done in terra cotta, and the name of each faculty member is again directly under his portrait. I think I should point out that Bill McVey was a former student in architecture, a former member of the faculty of that department, and most recently director of the Museum of Fine Arts in Cleveland, from which position he has retired. At the 1983 commencement he was honored as an outstanding alumnus. From left to right on the east wall are the portraits of Dr. Joseph I. Davies, formerly of biology; Dr. Carroll Camden, Professor Emeritus of English; and Dr. Claude Heaps, the man from whom all freshmen took Physics 100 over many years.

149
And then comes Dean Emeritus and Professor Emeritus of Chemistry G. Holmes Richter, who still maintains an office in the Chemistry Building where he may be found daily.

150
Then we have the second president of the Institute, Dr. William V. Houston, who was also a physicist.

151
Next is Dr. Carey Croneis, who was provost and acting president of the university, as well as professor of geology.

152
Here is Dr. Thomas W. Bonner, for whom the Bonner Physical Laboratory was named. Dr. Floyd Ulrich, formerly professor of mathematics, is not shown, despite the fact that he was one of the most skilled billiard players on the faculty.

153
I do show Dr. Alan D. McKillop, who was one of the recipients of the Distinguished Professorships, his in English.

154
And beginning with the faculty portraits on the west wall is that of James "Jimmy" Chillman, Jr., who began teaching at Rice in 1917 and was ultimately appointed a Distinguished Professor of Fine Arts. He was also founder and former director of the Museum of Fine Arts in Houston and taught until he was eighty years old. Next comes Professor Emeritus of French, Dr. André Bourgeois (not shown here), and Dr. A. J. Hartsook, Professor Emeritus of Chemical Engineering (also not shown).

65

155
Another former Distinguished Professor was Dr. Hubert E. Bray, mathematician, humorist, and the other of the two most skilled billiard players. Dr. Bray received his Ph.D. from Rice in 1918 and taught until 1970.

156
Finally, we come to the first president, Edgar Odell Lovett, who was Mr. Rice Institute for many years. Later we will see the residential college that was named for him.

157
This is Dr. Floyd S. Lear, the last of the Distinguished Professors, in his case of course in history. Dr. Edgar Altenburg of biology, James S. Waters of electrical engineering, and Gilbert L. Hermance of physical education complete those on the west wall who are not shown. If you do some real searching around the exterior of the Cohen House, you may locate a pair of heads cut in stone. These are Anderson Todd and William Cannady, the architects in 1976 for less major alterations that eliminated the billards room and changed the library into a bar known as "George's Tavern."

Allen Center

158
On our way to Baker College, we stop by the north lobby of Allen Center, where a large, handsome stone owl is keeping watch over the business of the university. This is the work of Annie Coury.

Residential Colleges

When the residential college system was introduced in 1957, a major series of additions was made to East Hall (Baker College), South Hall (Will Rice College), West Hall (Hanszen College), and Wiess Hall. The latter was built in 1950, and Staub, Rather and Howze were the architects. When it was laid out, an error of two or three degrees was made, so that it is not parallel to the other buildings on campus. Additional living spaces were added to all of the new colleges except Wiess. New dining halls were added to all the colleges except for Baker, which already had one; and a master's residence was added to all four.

159
We begin our tour of the colleges at the east end of Baker College, built in 1914 and originally called East Hall. This is an unusual elevation, in that the columns are marble and there is both limestone and considerable brick. The areas of the wall that are stucco barely redeem the original philosophy regarding use of materials on residential buildings.

(See Color Plate 11.) On the newer wing of Baker College, we have four stone owls roosting, as it were, on four stone pilasters. The colorful mosaics were designed by James Chillman and were fabricated in Mexico. These mosaics are located in many other areas of Baker, and also on Will Rice and Hanszen Colleges. All the additions to the colleges that were new were the work of Wilson, Morris, Crain and Anderson, Architects.

160

This is the south cloister of Baker College, showing ten columns with very unusual capitals, with surprising quotations for a nonsectarian school. They come from the book of Proverbs in the Bible, and from the Wisdom of Solomon in the book of the Apocrypha, which is not included in most denominations' Bibles. The series begins on the first column on the left, closest to the commons, and had to be carved in sequence, as in some cases the quotations are too long to appear on just one capital. It was rather a neat trick to make the proverbs fit exactly on ten columns, especially since one side of columns 4 and 7 could not be used. The quotations begin on the west face and continue on the south, east, and north faces in order. Only the carving on the first column is shown.

On column 1 (from Wisdom of Solomon, Chapter 7, Verse 7):

161
I PRAYED & UNDERSTAND

162
ING WAS GIVEN ME. I CALL'D

163
UPON GOD & THE SPIRIT

164
OF WISDOM CAME UNTO ME.

On column 2 (Wisdom of Solomon, Chapter 7, Verses 25 and 26):

FOR WISDOM IS A BREATH
OF THE POWER OF GOD.
SHE IS THE REFLECTION OF
THE EVERLASTING LIGHT.

On column 3 (Verse 27):

IN ALL AGES ENTER
ING INTO HOLY SOULS
SHE MAKETH FRIENDS
OF GOD AND PROPHETS.

The quotations on columns 4 through 8 are sometimes used in Episcopal churches and perhaps others as the Old Testament reading for the eleventh Sunday after Pentacost.

On column 4 (Book of Proverbs, Chapter 9, Verse 1):

WISDOM HATH BUILDED
A.D. 1914 [where the downspout interfered]
HER HOUSE, SHE HATH HEWN
HER SEVEN PILLARS, SHE

On column 5 (Proverbs, Chapter 9, Verse 2):

HATH MINGLED HER WINE
SHE HATH ALSO FURNISH
ED HER TABLE SHE HATH
SENT FOR HER MAIDENS.

On column 6 (Verse 3):

SHE CRIETH UPON THE
HIGHEST PLACES OF THE
CITY, WHOSO IS SIMPLE
LET HIM TURN IN HITHER.

On column 7 (Verse 4):

AS FOR HIM THAT IS VOID

165
A.D. 1914 [another downspout]
OF UNDERSTANDING, SHE
SAITH TO HIM, COME EAT

On column 8 (Verses 5 and 6):

YE OF MY BREAD & DRINK
OF THE WINE WHICH I HAVE
MINGLED & WALK IN THE
WAY OF UNDERSTANDING.

On column 9 (Proverbs, Chapter 8, Verse 34):

BLESSED IS THE MAN
THAT HEARETH ME, WATCH
ING DAILY AT MY GATES
WAITING AT THE POSTS

On column 10 (Proverbs, Chapter 8, Verse 35):

OF MY DOORS, FOR WHOSO
FINDETH ME, FINDETH
LIFE AND SHALL OBTAIN
FAVOUR OF THE LORD.

166

We continue our tour with a view of the original "Faculty Tower," with its now inoperative clock. In earlier days unmarried members of the faculty often lived here. The large clock did operate then. The cloister at the right connects Baker College dining hall to the wing of Will Rice College that was known as South Hall; that was the first actual residential dormitory on campus. Note the single marble column magically located where a larger arch would not fit. There are now a total of eight colleges, whereas originally (in 1957) there were five, which included Jones, the first women's college.

167

Here is the exterior of the capital of the lonesome column, and another senior. The inside of this column also shows the head of a student, but one who must not be graduating.

(See Color Plate 12.) In the library of Baker College are several of the original lighting fixtures in stained glass, giving the designer another chance to use the Rice shield.

71

168
This early photograph shows Mr. Watkin supervising the laying of the cornerstone for South Hall. Note the campanile with the 1912 top in the background. You might also notice that the cornerstone does not appear to have been completed, as the date has not yet been carved on it: MDCCCCXII. As was his custom, Dr. Lovett wrote the inscription, which reads: TO THE FREEDOM OF SOUND LEARNING AND THE FELLOWSHIP OF YOUTH.

169
The very handsome south cloister of old Will Rice College makes one feel he is in Italy. This cloister forms the north side of a quadrangle enclosed on three sides by Will Rice College buildings.

170
Here is one of the floral capitals on that cloister.

171
Here begins a series of terra-cotta panels on Will Rice College dining hall and on the Hanszen College dining hall. These depict various aspects of student life in the 1920s. Bill McVey, a freshman in 1923 who received his degree in architecture in 1927, designed and made them with the help of Mrs. McVey, who was a ceramist of international stature, having exhibited extensively in the United States and many other countries. Three separate firings were required: one for the stoneware, a second (at lower temperatures) for

72

the color glazes, and a third when mosaics were used. The mosaics were imported from Florence, Italy. The ceramics were installed in 1957, but unfortunately Mr. McVey does not recall the exact significance of every one of the panels. I have not included photographs of the first two on the left: a student nervously anticipating a date, and an engineer with a slide rule. (Today, the engineering student might not know how to use a slide rule!) This student is writing home, undoubtedly for money.

172
Here is another student, studying catenary curves and towers and structures equations: probably a civil engineer.

173
The next panel is the freshman quarterback George Alexander "Granddaddy" Wood, who in 1924 completed a sixty-yard pass to "Red" Moore. George Wood was elected to the Rice Hall of Fame in 1983.

174
This is a freshman, very immature, from El Campo, wearing the "dink" required of first-year students in those days.

175
And an architectural student with T-square and triangle, no doubt burning the midnight oil.

176
A coed in Biology 100 dissects an unfortunate frog. Omitted is the next panel of a student studying the constellations, so you will have to come to the campus to see this very nice ceramic with its gold constellations.

177
A student rather sleepily resigns himself to missing his eight o'clock class, which happened (especially on Saturdays!) to many students in the days when the faculty were early risers and liked early classes. Not shown is the terra cotta of the young man who has a vision of the opposite sex, which shows what happens to good intentions to study. Book is closed!

178
This particularly wonderful panel shows Jesse Madden of the class of 1927 hoisting the freshman class president Bill McVey into the hidden spaces of the Turnverein Club. He reportedly spent two days hiding in the ceiling until the night of the sophomore prom, which he crashed by lowering himself down. Not shown is a baffled engineer, unable to solve the math problems furnished by Dr. Hubert Bray.

179
Here is Jack Glenn, a dedicated cheerleader and former *Rice Thresher* editor, who later became prominent in radio news reporting. He is shown against a background of mosaic tile, which Bill McVey called "smalti" and used to represent the color of a crowd in the background. Omitted are the senior who dreams of the diploma that is so near and yet so far; another student—who shall be nameless—who hated water in any form but gets a much-needed bath, probably in Hermann Park; and hamburgers, known as "hockey pucks," being served to unhappy diners by a student waiter.

180
There are five ceramic shields on the newer portion of Hanszen College. This first one is obvious; but the use of color is very nice indeed, and you should really make an effort to see it. Bill McVey did this Rice shield.

181
Another is the shield of Hanszen College, a very flamboyant design.

182
And another is the shield representing the arts, which I referred to earlier as being identical to the stone carving on Rayzor Hall. This one is much nicer!

183
Still another is the shield representing engineering.

184
Finally, the one representing science is on the south wall of one of the residential wings of the college and is very nicely done.

185
The terra-cotta panels on Hanszen College were done at the same time as those at Will Rice College, but a fire destroyed the original commons at Hanszen in the summer of 1975. No damage was done to the McVey terra cottas, but when the dining hall was rebuilt it was redesigned; and space for only sixteen ceramics was provided, instead of seventeen. The panel showing a sophomore paddling a freshman was omitted. It was broken at one time but was repaired by Dr. Stephen Baker, who was then master of Hanszen College; it is now in the archives. The panels on Hanszen are now set in a very dark glazed tile, rather than in the regular St. Joe brick.

77

186
The names of the graduating seniors are read, with those who are graduating "with distinction" or "with honors" in those days. It was only comparatively recently that the honors "cum laude," "magna cum laude," and "summa cum laude" have been awarded. Attendance of the faculty at commencement was mandatory, but some of the faculty wives were parked nearby, ready to leave the Houston summer heat as soon as the exercises were over. The first air conditioning on campus was installed when Fondren Library was built. In sequence, the panels not shown here are a relay runner, which has a lovely background of "smalti"; and a chemistry student with his laboratory apparatus.

187
Much poker was played in those days, and this sometimes led to enforced withdrawal from the Institute. Today the computer can become just as addictive as playing cards sometimes was then. Look carefully for the panel of the student writing a girl back home, with her picture providing the necessary inspiration, as well as the panel of the civil engineer surveying the campus for the millionth time and the panel of the baseball player "taking his cuts" with the crowd in the background.

188
A student studies French, a foreign language being an Institute requirement in those days. It hardly seemed necessary to include the next panel of "boy meets girl," this being typical of campus life at every university.

189
And here we have Bill McVey in Paris, with the Eiffel Tower in the background. In the lower right-hand corner is "To – E. J. O." Dr. Eugene Oberle felt that no architectural student's education was complete unless he traveled in Europe, and he personally arranged the finances that made it possible for McVey to do so. In McVey's words, "Skoal, Gene." It was about this time when the traveling fellowship was instituted in the Department of Architecture, with funds provided by the Archi-Arts Ball.

The next three panels are not shown here. The first is a student trying to decide on a major; the second shows a student with Sammy the owl; and the third appears to be a student who has a serious case of spring fever, or perhaps "thoughts lightly turn."

190
From the days of winning teams, we see a football substitute awaiting his big chance. The next two panels are a student comfortably settled in a Hardoi chair, undoubtedly making a long telephone call, and a biologist weary from chasing butterflies with his net.

191
This is the cloister of the dormitory built in 1916 and known then as West Hall. Today it is part of Hanszen College. This cloister helps to form the Hanszen quadrangle.

192
On the left of the cloister arches is a single arch that is more than reminiscent of some in Italy. The cornerstone is to the right of this arch and reads
O VISION OF THOSE EARLY DAYS. O SPIRIT OF OUR YEARS OF FAITH. O TRUTH AND JUSTICE IN ALLIANCE WITH FREEDOM SOUL OF ART AND SCIENCE AND BEAUTY. TRUTHS UNDYING WRAITH GO WITH OUR SONS ON ALL THEIR WAYS.

193
On the north side of the old portion of Hanszen College are two unusual unsymmetrical entrances. Here is one of them. The small objects below the tall window are shells, cut into the stone.

194
Here is the other entrance. Take a little time to study both of them. At first they appear the same, but they are really very different. If you turn around after you look at these you will see Wiess College. On the north side of the Wiess commons are two types of shields in stone: Rice shields and Wiess College shields.

195
Edgar Odell Lovett College was built in 1968. It was the second college in the form of a modest "high-rise," Brown College being the first. Brown was built in 1965, the architect being Alan Shepherd of Brown and Root. The architects for Lovett College were Wilson, Morris, Crain and Anderson. In this photograph, the dormitory portion is on the right and the commons is on the left.

196
The contemporary sculpture in the entry garden of the college was created by Jim Love and is really quite striking. The push bars on the commons doors are of wood and have little Rice shields carved on them.

197
Passing through the Lovett College garden, we see a more-than-modest frame cage that is the home of "Sammy," the Rice mascot. And here he is, austere and sleepy, as he should be in daylight. In real life he is more majestic than even the finest of the carved ones. In the 1940s owls both roosted and reproduced in the chemistry tower. Although they are no longer there, the students always seem to have a live one on hand to be carried on high to basketball and football games and other student rallies and functions.

198
The real multistory dormitory is Sid Richardson College. It is the only one of the colleges in which the master's residence is incorporated within the dormitory structure. It was designed by architects Neuhaus and Taylor and completed in 1971.

199
In the court between Jones College and Brown College is the bronze statue called "The Sisters," the work of the renowned Carl Milles. The water fountains follow a cycle from virtually obscuring the figures with spray to no spray on the figures at all, at which time the surrounding fountains are at their highest.

200
Here is a part of Jones College, namely Jones North. The college was completed in 1957 with Lloyd, Morgan and Jones as architects. This college also has a quadrangle contained on three sides by the dormitory wings and the commons. It used to be a very nice space; but the landscaping has made it difficult to feel the enclosure of the buildings, and equally hard to photograph them.

201
This is the Jones College shield in mosaic near the entrance to the dining hall.

Rice Stadium

202
From the colleges, walk or look across the parking lot to the 72,000-seat Rice Stadium. It was completed in 1950, nine months after the football team won the Cotton Bowl on January 1, 1950. This photograph shows the great hole in the ground created by Brown and Root, the contractors, who kept the associated architects, Milton McGinty and Lloyd, Morgan and Jones burning the night oil trying to keep the design and drawings ahead of construction. Rice Stadium was one of the first stadiums, if not *the* first, where the spectators entered at midlevel. The date of this photograph is March 1950. During construction many Houstonians followed the progress of the work by visiting the site every Sunday in response to a sign on Rice Boulevard that invited each and all to a fifty yard line construction observation seat.
(See Color Plate 13.) This stadium is truly a handsome piece of architecture. Here is a June 12, 1950, photograph of the fifty yard line upper stands. Funds for the construction of the stadium were raised by selling "options" to buy tickets in certain locations for a period of twenty years, plus funds accumulated by the Athletic Department. The original charter of the Institute prohibited borrowing funds for the construction of buildings, undoubtedly a wise limitation for a private university. As a result, the stadium was paid for upon completion.

83

203
The forms for the lower fifty yard line seats were literally bent to form the curved seats on the four "corners." This photo was also taken on June 12, 1950.

204
On September 3, 1950, only a few seats remained to be installed. The team entrance is located at the right or south end of the stadium; and the pumphouse, which keeps the surface from flooding, is at the north end of the field. The official opening matched Rice against Santa Clara, and fortunately the use of this facility began on a winning note, as Rice won 27 to 7.

I hope this tour also ends on a winning note. While you may feel that your visit has been complete, there are a minimum of two hundred other items worth seeing, including buildings that I have omitted. I have been looking over the campus for more than forty years now, and I find new points of interest almost every trip. Whether or not you return for more, I know that I shall! The possibilities of seeing are endless and will make for more and more enjoyment for us all.